MAPLE
PUBLISHERS

Du'a – The Essence of Tawhid

Author: Ramon Rizvi, Raza Rizvi & Zain Rizvi

Copyright © Ramon Rizvi, Raza Rizvi & Zain Rizvi (2023)

The right of Ramon Rizvi, Raza Rizvi & Zain Rizvi to be identified as author of this work has been asserted by the author in accordance with section 77 and 78 of the Copyright, Designs and Patents Act 1988.

First Published in 2023

ISBN 978-1-83538-047-5 (Paperback)
         978-1-83538-048-2 (Hardback)
         978-1-83538-049-9 (E-Book)

Book Layout, Cover Design, Copy-editing and Proofreading by:
      White Magic Studios
      www.whitemagicstudios.co.uk

Published by:
      Maple Publishers
      Fairbourne Drive, Atterbury,
      Milton Keynes,
      MK10 9RG, UK
      www.maplepublishers.com

A CIP catalogue record for this title is available from the British Library.

All rights reserved. No part of this book may be reproduced or translated by any form or by any means, electronic or mechanical, including photocopying, recording or by any information storage and retrieval system without written permission from the author.

The views expressed in this work are solely those of the author and do not reflect the opinions of Publishers, and the Publisher hereby disclaims any responsibility for them.

I would like to thank my elder brother for being a source of inspiration. Moreover, I would like to thank my wife for constantly challenging my views thus allowing me to refine my arguments more concisely.

Above all, I would like to thank Allah (SWT) for blessing me with a long enough life enabling me to search and find what I believe to be the truth.

Ramon Rizvi

Motivation: There has been much confusion within the Ummah around supplicating to the Prophets of Allah. Some argue that not only is it permissible but it is also recommended whilst others argue that it falls under the umbrella of shirk (associating partners with Allah). If this act invalidates the essence of Tawhid then Allah will make this crystal clear in the Quran.

*"It is He who has sent down to you, [O Muḥammad], the Book; **in it are verses precise – they are the foundation of the Book** - and others unspecific. As for those in whose hearts is deviation, they will follow that of it which is unspecific, seeking discord and seeking an interpretation [suitable to them]. And no one knows its interpretation except Allah..."*

Surah Al 'Imran 3 : 7

Contents

Tawhid

The following beliefs fall under the umbrella of His Majesty's Lordship

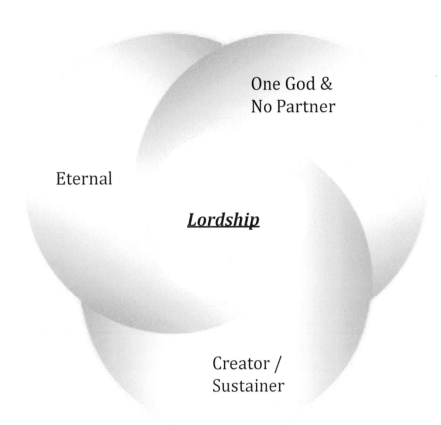

One God &
No Partner

Eternal

Lordship

Creator /
Sustainer

There is no God except Allah, He is the only deity

- **_Allah – there is no deity except Him_**. _To Him belong the best names_

  Surah Taha   20 : 8

- _So know, [O Muḥammad], that_ **_there is no deity except Allah_** _and ask forgiveness for your sin and for the believing men and believing women. And Allah knows of your movement and your resting place_

  Surah Muhammad   47 : 19

- _So exalted is Allah, the Sovereign, the Truth;_ **_there is no deity except Him_**_, Lord of the Noble Throne_

  Surah Al – Mu'minun   23 : 116

- **_Allah - there is no deity except Him_**_, the Ever-Living, the Self-Sustaining. Neither drowsiness overtakes Him nor sleep. To Him belongs whatever is in the heavens and whatever is on the earth. Who is it that can intercede with Him except by His permission? He knows what is [presently] before them and what will be after them, and they encompass not a thing of His knowledge except for what He wills. His Kursi extends over the heavens and the earth, and their preservation tires Him not. And He is the Most High, the Most Great_

  Surah Al – Baqarah   2 : 255 (Ayatul Kursi)

Allah is everlasting, He is eternal

- **_Whatever you have will end, but what Allah has is lasting._** And We will surely give those who were patient their reward according to the best of what they used to do

Surah An – Nahl 16 : 96

- *Allah,* **the Eternal Refuge**

Surah Al – Ikhlas 112 : 2

- **He neither begets nor is born**

Surah Al – Ikhlas 112 : 3

Allah is the creator of all things

- **Allah has created every creature** from water. And of them are those that move on their bellies, and of them are those that walk on two legs, and of them are those that walk on four. **Allah creates what He wills.** Indeed, Allah is over all things competent

Surah An – Nur   24 : 45

- She said, 'My Lord, how will I have a child when no man has touched me?' [The angel] said, 'Such is Allah; **He creates what He wills. When He decrees a matter, He only says to it, 'Be,' and it is'**

Surah Al 'Imran   3 : 47

- That is Allah, your Lord; there is no deity except Him, **the Creator of all things**, so worship Him. And He is Disposer of all things

Surah Al – An'am   6 : 102

- **Allah is the Creator of all things**, and He is, over all things, Disposer of affairs

Surah Az – Zumar   39 : 62

---

10   There are ayahs which also tell us "Allah is the Sustainer" (13:26, 62:11, 51:58 etc)

The following actions fall under the umbrella for worshipping Allah

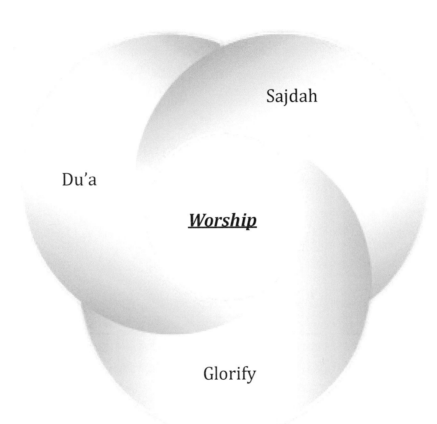

Other acts could also be considered to be a form of worship, however the focal point will be worshipping Allah through the process of du'a (supplication)

11

Allah equates the act of prostration with the act of worshipping

- *O Mary, be devoutly obedient to your Lord and **prostrate and bow with those who bow [in prayer]***

  Surah Al 'Imran   3 : 43

- *O you who have believed, **bow and prostrate and worship your Lord** and do good - that you may succeed*

  Surah Al – Hajj   22 : 77

- *Indeed, those who are near your Lord [i.e. the angels] are not prevented by arrogance from His **worship**, and they exalt Him, and to Him they **prostrate***

  Surah Al – A'raf   7 : 206

- *So **prostrate** to Allah and **worship** [Him]*

  Surah An – Najm   53 : 62

- *And establish **prayer** and give zakah and **bow with those who bow [in worship and obedience]***

  Surah Al – Baqarah   2 : 43

Exalting / Glorifying Allah is also considered a form of worship

- _Do you not see that Allah is exalted by whomever is within the heavens and the earth and [by] the birds with wings spread [in flight]? Each [of them] has known his [means of] **prayer and exalting** [Him], and Allah is knowing of what they do_

  Surah An – Nur   24 : 41

- _Indeed, those who are near your Lord [i.e., the angels] are not prevented by arrogance **from His worship, and they exalt Him**, and to Him they prostrate_

  Surah Al – A'raf   7 : 206

- _So **exalt [Allah] with praise of your Lord** and be of those who prostrate [to Him]. **And worship** your Lord until there comes to you the certainty [i.e. death]_

  Surah Al – Hijr   15 : 98-99

- _Say, 'Call upon Allah or call upon the Most Merciful. Whichever [name] you call - to Him belong the best names.' And do not recite [too] loudly in your **prayer** or [too] quietly but seek between that an [intermediate] way. And say, '**Praise to Allah**, who has not taken a son and has had no partner in [His] dominion and has no [need of a] protector out of weakness; **and glorify Him with [great] glorification**'_

  Surah Al – Isra   17 : 110-111

Certain praise is reserved for Allah alone, reciting such praise is an act of worship as it glorifies Allah

- *You cause the night to enter the day, and You cause the day to enter the night; and You bring the living out of the dead, and You bring the dead out of the living. And You give provision to whom You will without account [i.e., limit or measure]*

  Surah Al 'Imran 3 : 27

- *And it is He who sends down rain from the sky, and We produce thereby the growth of all things. We produce from it greenery from which We produce grains arranged in layers. And from the palm trees - of its emerging fruit are clusters hanging low. And [We produce] gardens of grapevines and olives and pomegranates, similar yet varied. Look at [each of] its fruit when it yields and [at] its ripening. Indeed in that are signs for a people who believe*

  Surah Al – An'am 6 : 99

- *Then, to Allah belongs [all] praise - Lord of the heavens and Lord of the earth, Lord of the worlds*

  Surah Al – Jathiyah 45 : 36

Du'a / Supplication is an act of worship

- *And your Lord says, '__Call upon Me__; I will respond to you.' Indeed, those who disdain My __worship__ will enter Hell contemptible*

    Surah Ghafir   40 : 60

- *And that the __masjids__ are for Allah, so do not __invoke__ with Allah anyone*

    Surah Al – Jinn   72 : 18

- *And when the people are gathered [that Day], __they [who were invoked]__ will be enemies to them, __and they will be deniers of their worship__*

    Surah Al – Ahqaf   46 : 6

- *Say, 'Indeed, I have been forbidden to __worship__ those you __invoke__ besides Allah.' Say, 'I will not follow your desires, for I would then have gone astray, and I would not be of the [rightly] guided'*

    Surah Al – An'am   6 : 56

Supporting narrations from Imam Jafar al Sadiq (AS) which prove du'a is an act of worship

- (1) Imam Jafar al Sadiq (AS) said the following: '***O Maysir, pray*** and do not say that it is predetermined and it is all over. There is a position with Allah, the Majestic, the Glorious, that is not accessible without praying to *Him*. ***If a servant keeps his mouth closed and does not plead to receive help, he will not receive anything.*** O Maysir, there is no door that is knocked repeatedly but that sooner or later it will open up'

  Graded (Sahih)

- (2) Imam Jafar al Sadiq (AS) said the following: "Allah, the Most Majestic, the Most Holy, has said, '*Those who consider themselves above the need to **worship** me will soon go to hell in disgrace* (40:60).' ***This is reference to du'a. The best form of worship is du'a (pleading before Allah for help)***"

  Graded (Sahih)

- (3) Imam Jafar al Sadiq (AS) was asked: '***Which form of worship is better?***' The Imam said, 'There is nothing more excellent before Allah, the Most Majestic, the Most Holy, than to ***ask and request Him*** to grant one from things He owns. Allah, the Most Majestic, the Most Holy, hates no one more than one who feels himself greater than to be in need of ***asking Allah for help***, thus, he does not ask Him for help.'

  Graded (Hasan)

Allah tells us to invoke him alone

- **And do not invoke besides Allah** *that which neither benefits you nor harms you, for if you did, then indeed you would be of the wrongdoers*

  Surah Yunus 10 : 106

- *Say, [O Muḥammad], 'My Lord has ordered justice and that you direct yourselves [to the Qiblah] at every place [or time] of* **prostration, and invoke Him***, sincere to Him in religion.' Just as He originated you, you will return [to life]*

  Surah Al – A'raf 7 : 29

- *Say, [O Muḥammad], '***I only invoke my Lord** *and do not associate with Him anyone'*

  Surah Al – Jinn 72 : 20

- *The example of those who take allies other than Allah is like that of the spider who takes [i.e., constructs] a home. And indeed, the weakest of homes is the home of the spider, if they only knew. Indeed, Allah knows* **whatever thing they call upon other than Him***. And He is the Exalted in Might, the Wise*

  Surah Al – Ankabut 29 : 41-42

There are clear examples in the Quran in which Allah is being supplicated to

- *At that, Zechariah __called upon his Lord, saying__, 'My Lord, grant me from Yourself a good offspring. Indeed, You are the Hearer of supplication'*

Surah Al 'Imran 3 : 38

- *__And Moses said__, 'Our Lord, indeed You have given Pharaoh and his establishment splendor and wealth in the worldly life, our Lord, that they may lead [men] astray from Your way. Our Lord, obliterate their wealth and harden their hearts so that they will not believe until they see the painful punishment.' [Allah] said, 'Your supplication has been answered__. So remain on a right course and follow not the way of those who do not know'*

Surah Yunus 10 : 88-89

- *When he __called to his Lord a private call [i.e. supplication]__. He said, 'My Lord, indeed my bones have weakened, and my head has filled with white, and never have I been in __my supplication to You__, my Lord, unhappy [i.e. disappointed]'*

Surah Maryam 19 : 3-4

- *And Noah, __when he called before, so We responded to him__ and saved him and his family from the great affliction*

Surah Al – Anbiya 21 : 76

Allah says he is the one who responds to the invocation of the supplicant

- *And your Lord says, 'Call upon Me;* **I will respond to you***.' Indeed, those who disdain My worship will enter Hell contemptible*

  Surah Ghafir   40 : 60

- ***Is He who responds to the desperate one when he calls upon Him*** *and removes evil and makes you inheritors of the earth? Is there a deity with Allah? Little do you remember*

  Surah An – Naml   27 : 62

- *And when My servants ask you, [O Muḥammad], concerning Me - indeed I am near.* **I respond to the invocation** *of the supplicant when he calls upon Me. So let them respond to Me [by obedience] and believe in Me that they may be [rightly] guided.*

  Surah Al – Baqarah   2 : 186

- *And Job, when he called to his Lord, 'Indeed, adversity has touched me, and You are the most merciful of the merciful.'* **So We responded to him** *and removed what afflicted him of adversity. And We gave him [back] his family and the like thereof with them as mercy from Us and a reminder for the worshippers [of Allah]*

  Surah Al – Anbya   21 : 83-84

The following are unique to Allah and they fall under the umbrella of His Majesty's divine attributes

All Seeing

All
Hearing

**_Divine
Attributes_**

Sole
Helper

Allah has other divine attributes however only the above three will be proven

Allah is all hearing and all seeing

- *[Allah] said, "Fear not. Indeed, I am with you both; **I hear and I see***

  Surah Taha 20 : 46

- *And you did not kill them, but it was Allah who killed them. And you threw not, [O Muḥammad], when you threw, but it was Allah who threw that He might test the believers with a good test. Indeed, **Allah is Hearing and Knowing***

  Surah Al – Anfal 8 : 17

- *Creator of the heavens and the earth. He has made for you from yourselves, mates, and among the cattle, mates; He multiplies you thereby. There is nothing like unto Him, **and He is the Hearing, the Seeing***

  Surah Ash – Shuraa 42 : 11

- *Certainly has Allah heard the speech of the one who argues [i.e., pleads] with you, [O Muḥammad], concerning her husband and directs her complaint to Allah. And Allah hears your dialogue; indeed, **Allah is Hearing and Seeing***

  Surah Al – Mujadila 58 : 1

Allah explicitly tells us He is our only helper

- *And Allah is most knowing of your enemies; and sufficient is Allah as an ally, **and sufficient is Allah as a helper***

  Surah An – Nisa 4 : 45

- *It is **You we worship** and **You we ask for help***

  Surah Al – Fatihah 1 : 5

- *But Allah is your protector, **and He is the best of helpers***

  Surah Al 'Imran 3 : 150

- *It is Allah who created the heavens and the earth and whatever is between them in six days; then He established Himself above the Throne. You have **not besides Him any protector** or any intercessor; so will you not be reminded?*

  Surah As – Sajdah 32 : 4

- *Indeed, to Allah belongs the dominion of the heavens and the earth; He gives life and causes death. And **you have not besides Allah any protector or any helper***

  Surah At – Tawbah 9 : 116

22 It is self-explanatory that the help being sought after is the help from across the curtain of ghaib (the unseen)

There are three categories which must be preserved in order to ascribe to Tawhid

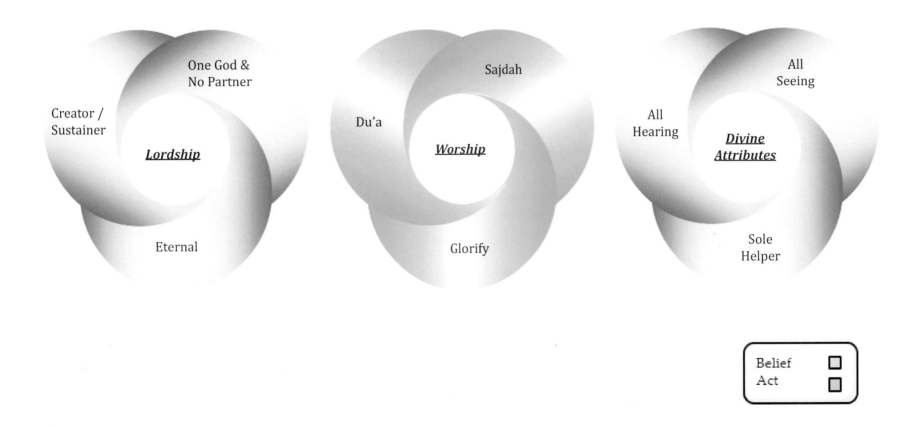

One God &
No Partner

Creator /
Sustainer

Lordship

Eternal

Sajdah

Du'a

Worship

Glorify

All
Seeing

All
Hearing

**_Divine
Attributes_**

Sole
Helper

Belief ☐
Act ☐

Since du'a is a form of worship it is self-explanatory that Allah alone should be invoked

Du'a – The Essence of Tawhid

His Majesty links together specific components from each category to ensure people do not supplicate to any other entity

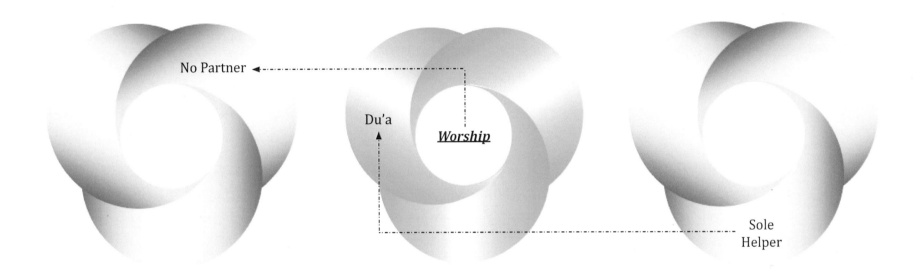

Allah restricts the act of supplication to an entity that can provide help

- **_And do not invoke besides Allah_** that which **_neither benefits you_** nor harms you, for if you did, then indeed you would be of the wrongdoers

  Surah Yunus   10 : 106

- And when **_adversity touches you at sea, lost are [all] those you invoke except for Him_**. But when He delivers you to the land, you turn away [from Him]. And ever is man ungrateful

  Surah Al – Isra   17 : 67

- O people, an example is presented, so listen to it. Indeed, **_those you invoke besides Allah_** will never create [as much as] a fly, even if they gathered together for it [i.e., that purpose]. **_And if the fly should steal from them a [tiny] thing, they could not recover it from him. Weak are the pursuer and pursued._**

  Surah Al – Hajj   22 : 73

- **_And those you call upon besides Him_** are unable to **_help you_**, nor can they help themselves

  Surah Al – A'raf   7 : 197

Allah compares the act of worshipping others with associating partners with Him

- *And [mention, O Muḥammad], the Day We will gather them all together - then **We will say to those who associated others with Allah**, '[Remain in] your place, you and your "partners".' Then We will separate them, and their "partners" will say, '**You did not used to worship us**, And sufficient is Allah as a witness between us and you **that we were of your worship unaware**'*

  Surah Yunus   10 : 28-29

- *And the Day He will gather them and that **which they worship besides Allah and will say**, 'Did you mislead these, My servants, or did they [themselves] stray from the way?' **They will say, 'Exalted are You! It was not for us to take besides You any allies [i.e. protectors]**. But You provided comforts for them and their fathers until they forgot the message and became a people ruined.' So they will deny you, in what you say, and you cannot avert [punishment] or [find] help. And whoever commits injustice among you - We will make him taste a great punishment*

  Surah Al – Furqan   25 : 17-19

- *The Messiah, son of Mary, was not but a messenger; [other] messengers have passed on before him. And his mother was a supporter of truth. They both used to eat food. Look how We make clear to **them the signs; then look how they are deluded**. Say, '**Do you worship besides Allah** that which holds for you no [power of] harm or benefit while it is Allah who is the Hearing, the Knowing?'*

  Surah Al - Ma'idah 5 : 75-76

In the above ayahs people were worshipping other people who had departed from this world

Seeking Help from across the curtain of ghaib is Du'a, and this results in Worship and Not Ascribing Partners

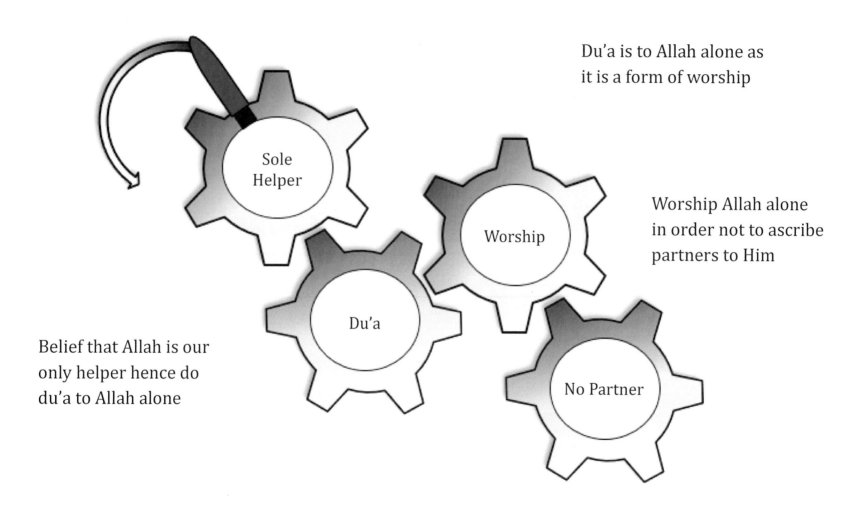

Du'a is to Allah alone as it is a form of worship

Worship Allah alone in order not to ascribe partners to Him

Belief that Allah is our only helper hence do du'a to Allah alone

The four components function together in perfect unison

To reinforce this notion, His Majesty links all four components from each of the three categories together

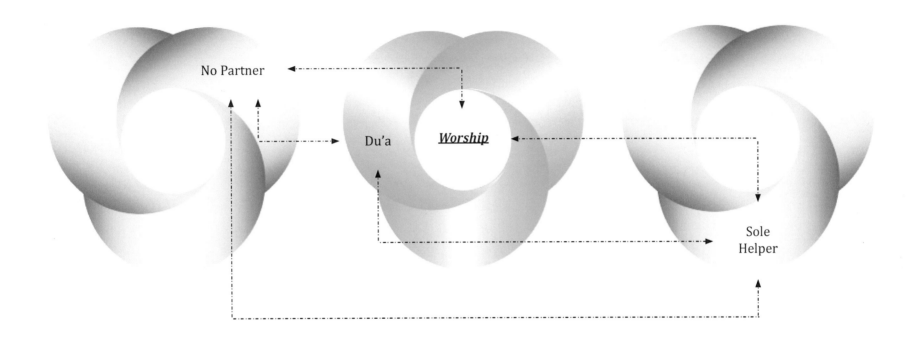

Allah restricts the act of worship to an entity that can provide help

- **_It is You we worship and You we ask for help_**

Surah Al – Fatihah   1 : 5

- But they **worship** rather than Allah that which does **not benefit them** or harm them, and the disbeliever is ever, against his Lord, an assistant [to Shaitan]

Surah Al – Furqan   25 : 55

- He said, "Then do you **worship** instead of Allah that which does **not benefit you** at all or harm you?

Surah Al – Anbya   21 : 66

- Say, "Do you **worship** besides Allah that which holds for you **no [power of] harm or benefit** while it is Allah who is the Hearing, the Knowing?"

Surah Al - Ma'idah   5 : 76

Allahs divine attribute of being our sole helper is unique to Him hence only he can be worshipped

Allah compares the act of invoking others to associating partners with Him

- _He causes the night to enter the day, and He causes the day to enter the night and has subjected the sun and the moon - each running [its course] for a specified term. That is Allah, your Lord; to Him belongs sovereignty._ ___And those whom you invoke other than Him___ _do not possess the membrane of a date seed._ ___If you invoke them,___ _they do not hear your supplication; and if they heard, they would not respond to you. And on the Day of Resurrection_ ___they will deny your association___. _And none can inform you like [one] Aware [of all matter]_

  **Surah Fatir   35 : 13-14**

- _Say, 'Have you considered: if there came to you the punishment of Allah or there came to you the Hour - is it_ ___other than Allah you would invoke,___ _if you should be truthful?' No, it is Him [alone] you would invoke, and He would remove that for which you invoked Him if He willed,_ ___and you would forget what you associate [with Him]___.

  **Surah Al – Anam   6 : 40-41**

- _And when_ ___those who associated others with Allah see their "partners,"___ _they will say, 'Our Lord, these are our partners whom we used_ ___to invoke besides You___.' _But they will throw at them the statement, 'Indeed, you are liars.' And they will impart to Allah that Day [their] submission, and lost from them is what they used to invent_

  **Surah An – Nahl   16 : 86-87**

In the ayahs quoted from Surah Fatir & Surah Nahl, people whom had passed away were being invoked

Allah compares the act of seeking help from other entities with associating partners with Him

- He invokes instead of Allah that which **neither harms him nor benefits him**. That is what is the **extreme error**. He invokes one whose harm is closer than his benefit - **how wretched the protector and how wretched the associate**

Surah Al – Hajj   22 : 12-13

- Say, 'Invoke those you have **claimed [as gods] besides Him, for they do not possess the [ability for] removal of adversity from you or [for its] transfer [to someone else]**.' Those whom they invoke seek means of access to their Lord, [striving as to] which of them would be nearest, and they hope for His mercy and fear His punishment. Indeed, the punishment of your Lord is ever feared

Surah Al – Isra   17 : 56-57

- Is He who responds to the desperate one when he calls upon Him **and removes evil** and makes you inheritors of the earth? **Is there a deity with Allah**? Little do you remember. Is He [not best] who guides you through the darknesses of the land and sea and who sends the winds as good tidings before His mercy? **Is there a deity with Allah? High is Allah above whatever they associate with Him**

Surah An – Naml   27 : 62-63

A crystal clear recurring theme in the Quran is the association of these four components with one another

Say, [O Muḥammad], "Have you considered that which you **invoke** besides Allah? Show me what they have created of the earth; or did they have **partnership in [creation of] the heavens**? Bring me a scripture [revealed] before this or a [remaining] trace of knowledge, if you should be truthful." And who is more astray than he who invokes besides Allah **those who will not respond to him until the Day of Resurrection, and they, of their invocation, are unaware**. And when the people are gathered [that Day], they [who were invoked] will be enemies to them, and they will be deniers of their **worship**.

Surah Al – Ahqaf 46 : 4-6

A strong dynamic bond coexists between these components forming a closed system

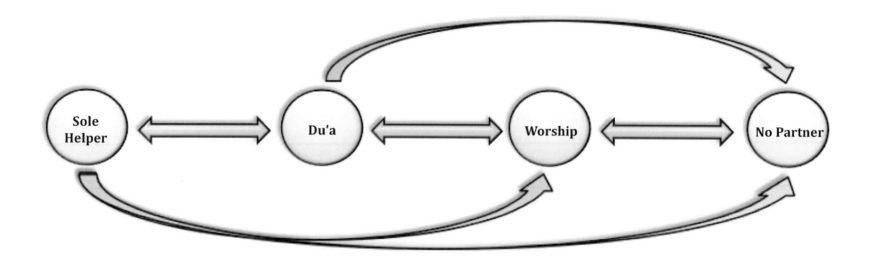

The synergy within this closed system is equivalent to that of an atom, it is impossible to separate any one of the components from the other three

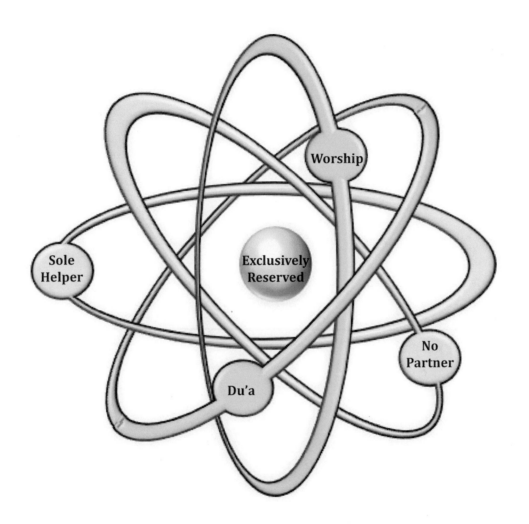

**Du'a to Allah alone is the ultimate declaration of adhering to Tawhid because it simultaneously preserves the unity across His Majesty's Lordship, Worship & Divine Attributes**

Proof by contradiction

The act of supplicating to another entity leads to one of two paths, both of which have a catastrophic outcome

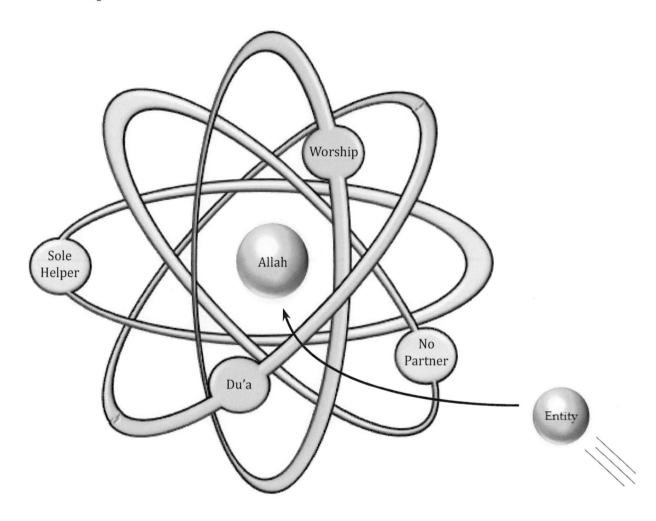

Path 1) Accept that the entity has now become a God

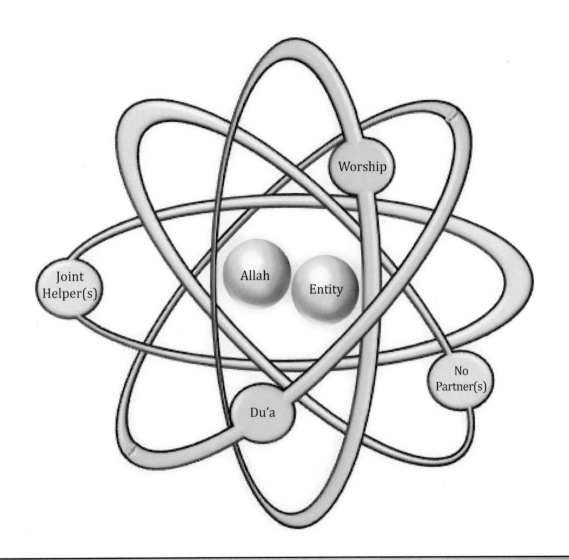

This is why when people were supplicating to other entities, Allah explicitly tells them they cannot help you & commands them to stop worshipping others / ascribing partners to Him & compares the entity to Himself

Path 2) Accept that the entity is part of Allah which results in a Demigod

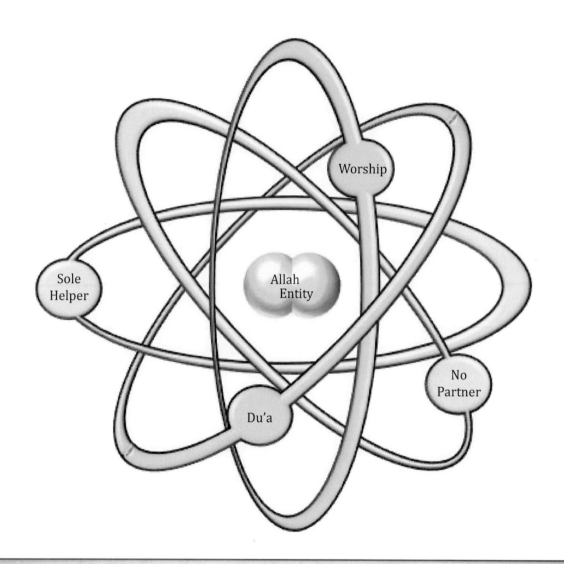

Christians believe in the Holy Trinity and this belief stems from the act of supplicating to other entities

<u>Du'a to anyone except Allah invalidates the sanctity of Tawhid because it instantaneously breaks the unity across His Majesty's Lordship, Worship & Divine Attributes</u>

Root cause of unintentional shirk

It is insufficient to have belief in Allah's lordship whilst breaking the unity of Allah's worship / divine attributes

- **And they worship other than Allah** that which neither harms them nor benefits them, and they say, **'These are our intercessors with Allah.'** Say, 'Do you inform Allah of something He does not know in the heavens or on the earth?' **Exalted is He and high above what they associate with Him**

  Surah Yunus 10 : 18

- And if you asked them, 'Who created the heavens and the earth?' **they would surely say, 'Allah.' Say, 'Then have you considered what you invoke besides Allah**? If Allah intended me harm, are they removers of His harm; or if He intended me mercy, are they withholders of His mercy?' Say, 'Sufficient for me is Allah; upon Him [alone] rely the [wise] reliers'

  Surah Az – Zumar 39 : 38

- And if you should ask them, 'Who has created the heavens and the earth?' **they would surely say, 'They were created by the Exalted in Might, the Knowing.'... But they have attributed to Him from His servants a portion**. Indeed, man is clearly ungrateful

  Surah Az – Zukhruf 43 : 9-15

People who had belief in Allah's lordship were still being scrutinised by Allah Himself, they were called "deluded" and had a lack of "reasoning" (29 : 61-63)

Such people attempted to redefine Tawhid by claiming other entities were "dependent" on Allah, this idea was used as a Quranic override so they can supplicate to other entities without worshipping & ascribing partners to them

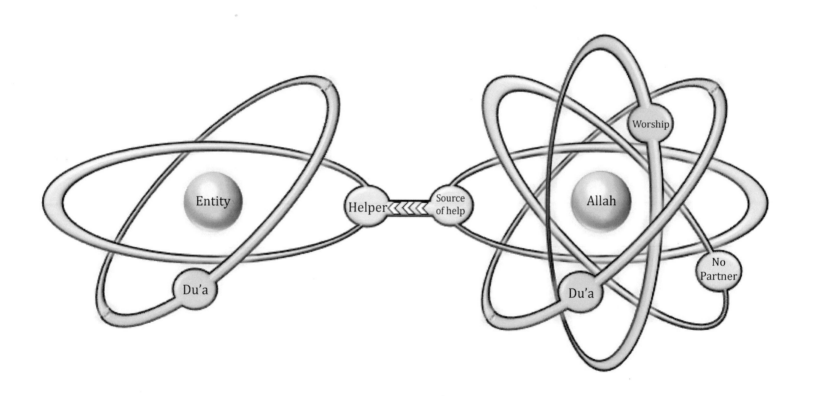

Du'a to others – An unfalsifiable belief

Summary of evidence for supplicating to Allah alone & Him being our sole helper

Aspect of Tawhid	Unequivocal ayahs that prove this aspect of Tawhid
Allah is our only helper	• We should seek help from Allah (alone) just like we worship Him (alone) (1 : 5) • Allah is a sufficient helper (4 : 45) • We have no helper except for Allah (9 : 116) • Others cannot help hence do not invoke them (10 : 106) • Calling upon others for help is associating partners with Allah (27 : 62-63) • Other people do not possess any power at all so do not seek help from them (35 : 13-14) • Prophet Isa & his mother (Mary) cannot help us (5 : 75-76)
Du'a is to Allah alone	• Du'a is to Allah alone (72 : 20) • Du'a is a form of worship (40 : 60) • All the du'a done by the Prophets from the Quran are to Allah alone (i.e. 3 : 38) • Only Allah can respond to our supplication (2 : 186) • Those who do du'a to others are condemned (29 : 41-42) • Those who invoke other people are condemned (46 : 4-6) • Invoking (worshipping) Prophet Isa or his mother (Mary) is condemned (5 : 75-76) • Belief in only 1 God whilst invoking others is condemned (39 : 38) • Invoking others is associating partners with Allah (16 : 86-87) • Those who blindly follow scholars and invoke others are being condemned (7 : 37-41) • Other people cannot hear or respond to our supplication (35 : 13-14) • Invoking others with the intent of seeking nearness to Allah is condemned (17 : 56-57) • Invoking others as intercessors / mediators is condemned (10 : 18)

46 Can you think of another ayah that Allah could have revealed in order to tell us, He is our only helper & du'a is to Him alone?

The sufficient evidence for invoking Allah alone is deemed as "insufficient" to those who supplicate to others

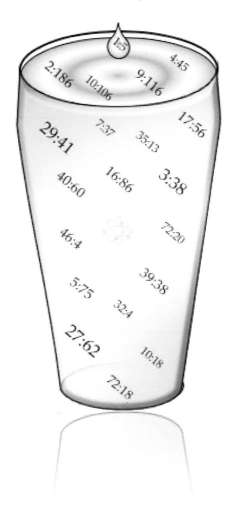

The clear ayahs which provide a mandate for Tawhid are constantly being evaded

72 : 20
- Ramon: This ayah tells us to invoke only Allah
- Sheikh: This is directed at idol worshippers only
- Ramon: With this reasoning can someone read the entire Quran and still invoke the sun?

1 : 5
- Ramon: This ayah tells us to seek help from Allah alone (just like we worship Him alone)
- Sheikh: Then we cannot seek help from other people for any means i.e. help in our daily lives
- Ramon: The ayah obviously refers to the help we are seeking from across the curtain of ghaib

39 : 38
- Ramon: This ayah condemns those who believe in Allah yet invoke others
- Sheikh: These people had the intention of doing du'a of worship not du'a of supplication
- Ramon: The Quran doesn't differentiate between du'a of worship / supplication, so why do you?

10 : 18
- Ramon: This ayah tells us that we cannot worship Allah via intercessors
- Sheikh: The intercessors used here were not Prophets of Allah
- Ramon: Allah would have then condemned using intercessors which are non-Prophets, but He didn't

The clear ayahs which provide a mandate for Tawhid are constantly being evaded

5 : 75-76
- Ramon: This ayah tells us Prophet Isa cannot help us
- Sheikh: These people believed that Prophet Isa was the son of God
- Ramon: The ayah doesn't say he refused to help due to their belief, it says he cannot help

35 : 13-14
- Ramon: This ayah tells us that other people cannot help / hear / respond to our du'a
- Sheikh: The Prophets are "dependent" on Allah so they can help / hear / respond to our du'a
- Ramon: This preconceived belief goes against the ayah itself

42 : 11
- Ramon: This ayah tells us that Allah alone is all hearing / seeing as these are His divine attributes
- Sheikh: The Prophets are "dependent" on Allah so they can hear / see us
- Ramon: This preconceived belief goes against the ayah itself

67 : 13
- Ramon: This ayah tells us that Allah alone is aware of our silent du'a (du'a recited in our minds)
- Sheikh: The Prophets are "dependent" on Allah so they are aware of our silent du'a
- Ramon: This preconceived belief goes against the ayah itself

The Prophets have become all hearing / seeing / helping / knowing, however this still doesn't invalidate Tawhid because it is caveated with the clause "with Allah's permission". With such a caveat nothing can be shirk

The invoking of Prophets has become a somewhat unfalsifiable belief

Unfalsifiable belief

- Ramon: What would constitute as "sufficient evidence", so that you invoke Allah (alone) and no one else?

- Sheikh: An ayah that says, We should not invoke any person irrespective of the following:

1) Using statues
2) The type of du'a being done
3) The person being a Prophet or not
4) Our personal beliefs about that specific Prophet
5) Dependency on Allah

- Ramon: Deriving Tawhid from a very specific preconceived belief which the Quran does not negate is nonsensical. With this reasoning anyone can believe in anything i.e. the Quran does not negate that the Prophets created the universe hence, they must have created the universe. Instead, we should take a Quran centric approach and derive Tawhid from the clear ayahs

Consequence of shirk

Making false claims upon Allah has severe ramifications

- ***And who is more unjust than he who invents a lie about Allah?*** *Those will be presented before their Lord, and the witnesses will say, 'These are the ones who lied against their Lord.'* ***Unquestionably, the curse of Allah is upon the wrongdoers***

  Surah Hud 11 : 18

- *Unquestionably, to Allah belongs whoever is in the heavens and whoever is on the earth.* ***And those who invoke other than Allah*** *do not [actually] follow [His] 'partners'.* ***They follow not except assumption, and they are not but misjudging***

  Surah Yunus 10 : 66

- *And do not say about what your tongues assert of untruth, 'This is lawful and this is unlawful,' to invent falsehood about Allah.* ***Indeed, those who invent falsehood about Allah will not succeed. [It is but] a brief enjoyment, and they will have a painful punishment***

  Surah An – Nahl 16 : 116-117

To convey how significant instilling a lie is upon His Majesty, Allah even threatens Prophet Muhammed (PBUH) if he was to invent a false saying (69:44, 17:73)

Allah threatens those who invent lies about his religion in order to invoke others

- _And who is more **unjust than one who invents about Allah a lie or denies His verses**? Those will attain their portion of the decree until, when Our messengers [i.e. angels] come to them to take them in death, they will say, **'Where are those you used to invoke besides Allah**?' They will say, 'They have departed from us,' and will bear witness against themselves that they were disbelievers. [Allah] will say, 'Enter among nations which had passed on before you of jinn and mankind into the Fire.' Every time a nation enters, it will curse its sister until, when they have all overtaken one another therein, the last of them will say about the first of them, **'Our Lord, these had misled us, so give them a double punishment of the Fire.' He will say, 'For each is double, but you do not know**.' And the first of them will say to the last of them, 'Then you had not any favour over us, so taste the punishment for what you used to earn.' Indeed, those who deny Our verses and are arrogant toward them - **the gates of Heaven will not be opened for them, nor will they enter Paradise until a camel enters into the eye of a needle [i.e., never]**. And thus do We recompense the criminals. They will have from Hell a bed and over them coverings [of fire]. And thus do We recompense the wrongdoers_

  **Surah Al – A'raf 7 : 37-41**

Blindly following scholars cannot be used as an excuse on the day of Judgement

- *And those who disbelieved will [then] say, 'Our Lord, show us those who misled us of the jinn and men [so] we may put them under our feet that they will be among the lowest'*

  ### *Surah Fussilat   41 : 29*

- *And when they will argue within the Fire, and the weak will say to those who had been arrogant, 'Indeed, we were your followers, so will you relieve us of a share of the Fire?' Those who had been arrogant will say, 'Indeed, all [of us] are in it. Indeed, Allah has judged between the servants'*

  ### *Surah Ghafir   40 : 47-48*

- *They have taken their scholars and monks as lords besides Allah, and [also] the Messiah, the son of Mary. And they were not commanded except to worship one God; there is no deity except Him. Exalted is He above whatever they associate with Him*

  ### *Surah At – Tawbah   9 : 31*

Shirk is the biggest sin and also an unforgivable sin

- Indeed, **Allah does not forgive association with Him**, but He forgives what is less than that for whom He wills. And he who associates others with Allah has certainly fabricated a **tremendous sin**

  Surah An – Nisa 4 : 48

- And We gave to him [i.e., Abraham] **Isaac and Jacob** - all We guided. And **Noah**, We guided before; and among his descendants, **David and Solomon** and **Job and Joseph and Moses and Aaron**. Thus do We reward the doers of good. And **Zechariah and John and Jesus and Elias** - and all were of the righteous. **And Ishmael and Elisha and Jonah and Lot** - and all We preferred over the worlds. And [some] among their fathers and their descendants and their brothers - and We chose them and We guided them to a straight path. That is the guidance of Allah by which He guides whomever He wills of His servants. **But if they had associated others with Allah, then worthless for them would be whatever they were doing**

  Surah Al – An'am 6 : 84-88

- Indeed, **Allah does not forgive association with Him**, but He forgives what is less than that for whom He wills. And he who associates others with Allah has certainly gone far astray. They call upon instead of Him none but female deities, and they actually call upon none but a rebellious Shaitan

  Surah An – Nisa 4 : 116-117

Committing shirk despite it being unintentional will not be accepted as an excuse on the day of Judgement

- (7) Imam Jafar al Sadiq (AS) was asked about the ayah of the Quran: *"To Allah belongs the conclusive argument"* **(6:149)**. Imam responds with, 'Allah will say to a slave on the day of Judgement: My slave did you possess knowledge? So if he says: yes, He will say to him: why did you not act by what you knew? And if he says: I was ignorant, He will say to him: why did you not seek knowledge so you could act? Thus he will be vanquished – and that is the "conclusive argument".'

  Graded (Sahih)*

- *Allah will say 'Throw into Hell every obstinate disbeliever, Preventer of good, aggressor, and doubter,* **Who made [as equal] with Allah another deity**; *then throw him into the severe punishment.' His [devil] companion will say, 'Our Lord, I did not make him transgress, but he [himself] was in extreme error.'* **Allah will say, 'Do not dispute before Me, while I had already presented to you the threat [i.e. warning]. The word [i.e., decree] will not be changed with Me, and never will I be unjust to the servants'**

  Surah Qaf 50 : 24-29

- *And [mention, O Muḥammad], the Day We will gather them all together; then We will say to those who associated others with Allah, 'Where are your 'partners' that you used to claim [with Him]?' Then there will be no [excuse upon] examination except they will say,* **'By Allah, our Lord, we were not those who associated.' See how they will lie about themselves. And lost from them will be what they used to invent**

  Surah Al – An'am 6 : 22-24

*The chain of narrators can be found in the appendix

And the Day He will call them and say, 'Where are My "partners" which you used to claim?' And We will extract from every nation a witness and say, 'Produce your proof,' and they will know that the truth belongs to Allah, and lost from them is that which they used to invent

Surah Al – Qasas   28 : 74-75

Appendix

- **(1) Al-Kafi volume 2, authenticated by Allamah Baqir al-Majlisi in Mir'at al-Uqul:** Abu Ali al-Ash'ari has narrated from Muhammad ibn 'Abd al-Jabbar from Safwan from Maysir ibn 'Abd al-'Aziz from Abu 'Abd Allah (a.s) who said the following: "Abu 'Abd Allah (a.s.) once said to me, 'O Maysir, **pray and do not say that it is predetermined and it is all over**. There is a position with Allah, the Majestic, the Glorious, that is not accessible without praying to Him. **If a servant keeps his mouth closed and does not plead to receive help, he will not receive anything**. O Maysir, there is no door that is knocked repeatedly but that sooner or later it will open up.'"

  Graded (Sahih)

- **(2) Al-Kafi volume 2, authenticated by Allamah Baqir al-Majlisi in Mir'at al-Uqul:** Ali ibn Ibrahim has narrated from his father from Hammad ibn 'Isa from Hariz from Zurara from Abu Ja'far (a.s) who said the following: "Allah, the Most Majestic, the Most Holy, has said, '*Those who consider themselves above the need to worship me will soon go to hell in disgrace.*' (40:60). The Imam said, 'This is reference to du'a. **The best form of worship is du'a (pleading before Allah for help)**' I (the narrator) then asked, 'What is meant by: Ibrahim is la awwahu, prayerful and forbearing?' The Imam said, '**It means pleading for help before Allah**.'"

  Graded (Sahih)

- **(3) Al-Kafi volume 2, authenticated by Allamah Baqir al-Majlisi in Mir'at al-Uqul:** Muhammad ibn Yahya has narrated from Ahmad ibn Muhammad from Muhammad ibn 'Isma'il and ibn Mahbub al Hanan ibn Sadir from his father who has said the following: "Once I asked abu Ja'far (a.s) '***Which form of worship is better***?'. The Imam said, 'There is nothing more excellent before Allah, the Most Majestic, the Most Holy, than to ***ask and request Him*** to grant one from things He owns. Allah, the Most Majestic, the Most Holy, hates no one more than one who feels himself greater than to be in need of ***asking Allah for help, thus, he does not ask Him for help***.'"

Graded (Hasan)

- **(4) Al-Kafi volume 2, authenticated by Allamah Baqir al-Majlisi in Mir'at al-Uqul:** Abu Ali al-Ash'ari has narrated from Muhammad ibn 'Abd al-Jabbar from ibn abu Najran from Sayf al-Tammar who said the following: "I heard abu 'Abd Allah (a.s.) saying, '***You must plead before Allah for help; you cannot seek nearness to Allah by any means better than pleading before Him for help. Do not leave your small needs without pleading before Allah for help***, just because they are small; both small and large needs are in the hands of One and the same One'."

Graded (Sahih)

- **(5) Imam Ali (a.s) in Nahjul Balagha, Sermon 110 (The best means to seek nearness to Allah):** The best means by which seekers of nearness to Allah, the Glorified, the Exalted, seek nearness, is the belief in Him and His Prophet, fighting in His cause, for it is the high pinnacle of Islam, and (to believe) in the kalimatu'l-'ikhlas (the expression of Divine purification) for it is just nature and the establishment of prayer for it is (the basis of) community, payment of zakat (Islamic tax) for it is a compulsory obligation, fasting for the month of Ramadan for it is the shield against chastisement, the performance of hajj of the House of Allah (i. e . Ka'bah) and its 'umrah' (other than annual visit) for these two acts banish poverty and wash away sins, regard for kinship for it increases wealth and length of life, to giving alms secretly for it covers shortcomings, giving alms openly for it protects against a bad death and extending benefits (to people) for it saves from positions of disgrace.

- **(6) Imam Ali (a.s) in Nahjul Balagha, Letter 31 (The last will of Ali ibn Abi Talib & Advice to one of his sons):** ... Leap into dangers for the sake of right wherever it be. Acquire insight into religious law. Accustom yourself to endure hardships since the best trait of character is endurance in matters of right. _**In all affairs resign yourself to Allah, because you will thus be resigning yourself to a secure shelter and a strong protector. You should ask only from your Lord because in His hand is all the giving and depriving. Seek good (from Allah) as much as you can.**_ Understand my advice and do not turn away from it, because the best saying is that which benefits. Know that there is no good in that knowledge which does not benefit, and if knowledge is not made use of then its acquisition is not justified... _**He has commanded you to beg from Him in order that He may give you**_ and to seek His mercy in order that He may have mercy on you. _**He has not placed anything between you and Him that may veil Him from you. He has not required you to get a mediator for you to Him,**_ and if you err, He has not prevented you from repentance.

- **(7) Mu'jam al-Ahadith al-Mu'tabara , authenticated by Sheikh Muhammad Asif Al-Mohseni:** al - Mufid from Ibn Qulawayh from Muhammad al - Himyari from his father from Harun from Ibn Ziyad who said: I heard Ja'far b. Muhammad (a.s) - and he was asked about His words the Exalted: '***To Allah belongs the conclusive argument!' (6:149)***, - say: 'Allah the Exalted will say to a slave on the day of Judgement: My slave did you possess knowledge? So if he says: yes, He will say to him: why did you not act by what you knew? ***And if he says: I was ignorant, He will say to him: why did you not seek knowledge so you could act? Thus he will be vanquished – and that is the "conclusive argument".***

Graded (Sahih)

Milton Keynes UK
Ingram Content Group UK Ltd.
UKRC040005241223
434841UK00001B/3

9 781835 380475